OFF THE RAILS

71

OFF THE RAILS

PATRICK WRIGHT

David & Charles
Newton Abbot   London   North Pomfret (Vt)

British Library Cataloguing in Publication Data
Wright, Patrick
   Off the rails.
   1. English wit and humour, Pictorial
   2. Railroads—Caricatures and cartoons
   I. Title
   741.5′942   NC1479

ISBN 0–7153–8620–4

Illustrations © Patrick Wright 1985

Phototypeset by ABM Typographics Limited, Hull
and printed in Great Britain
by Redwood Burn Ltd, Trowbridge, Wilts
for David & Charles (Publishers) Limited
Brunel House Newton Abbot Devon

Published in the United States of America
by David & Charles Inc
North Pomfret Vermont 05053 USA

For Jack King

Publisher's Note

We gricers, you know, sometimes treat ourselves too seriously, measuring our personal stature by the number of cylinder bores we memorise correctly to the exact millimetre. Bores did I say? 'Do you know number 54X3QZ worked the 2349 last night?' we mutter in our dirty gaberdine macks of regulation colour. 'You don't say.'

Well, of course, gricing is a serious business. I mean, who can really be surprised that a Plymouth friend was recently knocked up at 12.15am to be told to dash down to the station (whence he had just returned after completing an evening duty) because the Paddington sleeper was triple-headed. Just a shade unfortunate that he was in a deep sleep and the whole street was woken up by the hammering on the door, before his mother popped her head out of the window wondering what disaster had overtaken them. But, very understandably, because nobody remembers when that sleeper was last triple-headed; or could guess when BR would show such benevolence again.

But everything has its funny side, and the more human among we gricers do sometimes laugh at our hobby (or is it obsession?). And here is a book to cut us to size. You won't be surprised to hear that it did not arrive via our railway editor. It will probably be classified as humour rather than railways. It might even be bought by those who would turn their noses up at *real* railway books, like our snappily-named *The Londonderry & Lough Swilly Railway: A History of the Narrow Gauge Railways of North West Ireland Part Two* (currently out of print but we hope shortly to be reprinted).

Whether you are a committed gricer or an ordinary mortal who does not fully comprehend the finer points of gricing (and may even need to be told that the American equivalent of a gricer is a railroad buff), be prepared to chuckle. Patrick Wright's work is fun. He puts everyone down; he portrays the absurd with the message that it is only the truth slightly exaggerated; he catches many aspects and moods of the railway enthusiast and preservation business. And there is often far more than first meets the eye, slapstick and subtlety.

You will all have favourites. Mine (and I'm begging the original by way of compensation for the fact that the Cornish Riviera Express slipped past my office unnoticed while I was laughing) is the first one in the 'At Home' section. Again, utterly absurd but how little exaggeration.

I hope you enjoy it.

DAVID ST JOHN THOMAS

On the Rails

Toys and Models

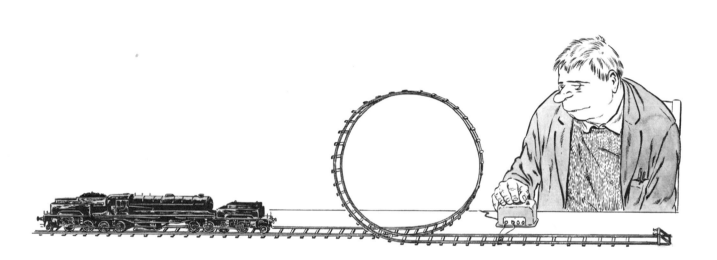

HAVE YOU USED MY COPY OF THIS MONTH'S 'RAILWAY MODELLER' FOR THE CAT'S DIRT BOX AGAIN, DOROTHY!
RAILWAY MODELLER

Off the Rails

THE FLYING SCOTSMAN.

THE WHEEL-TAPPER'S NIGHTMARE.

Steamers

At Home

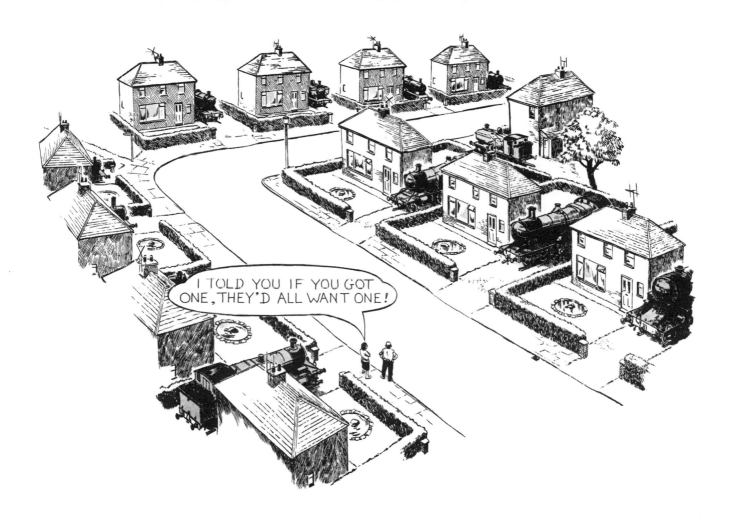

And Finally . . .

£6.95